D1636136

Today Is Great!

A DAILY
GRATITUDE JOURNAL
FOR KIDS

By Vicky Perreault

ROCKRIDGE
PRESS

Interior and Cover Designer: Suzanne LaGasa
Photo Art Director: Sara Feinstein
Editor: Kristen Depken
Production Editor: Ashley Polikoff
Illustrations: © Revelstock Art/Creative Market; Studio Desset/Creative Market; Invisible Layer/Creative Market.
Author Photo Courtesy of © Bella Iranitalab.

ISBN: Print 978-1-64152-882-5

THIS BOOK BELONGS TO

-------------------- .

Hello

INTRODUCTION

Have you ever felt gratitude before? Gratitude is noticing the good things in life and being thankful for them. One of the best ways to do this is by writing in a gratitude journal every day. Between school, homework, and activities, you may not always have time to notice the big and small moments of life. But even on the yuckiest of days, there is something to be grateful for, like a smile or a hug.

That's where this daily gratitude journal comes in. Every day, you'll have space to list the one thing you're most grateful for, such as seeing a rainbow or hanging out with a friend. You can use words, phrases, or sentences. How you write isn't important. What's important is that you get in the habit of writing. Try to write in your journal at the same time each day, maybe after school or before bed.

This journal also has weekly questions that will take more time. You can save those for the weekend. These questions will get you thinking about gratitude in a new way. Every other week, you'll get to take on a gratitude challenge. These are fun ways to promote kindness and spread gratitude. To keep you motivated, there are also positive quotes from some pretty smart people for you to read and share.

It takes just a few minutes a day to build your gratitude muscle. When you do, you'll start noticing more things to appreciate each day, and you may feel happier and more hopeful. Now **that** is something to write about!

Today I'm grateful for . . .

MONDAY

___ / ___ / ___

TUESDAY

___ / ___ / ___

WEDNESDAY

___ / ___ / ___

THURSDAY

___ / ___ / ___

FRIDAY

___ / ___ / ___

SATURDAY

___ / ___ / ___

SUNDAY

___ / ___ / ___

Name one special talent you have. How do you use it?

GRATITUDE CHALLENGE!

Write a thank you note to someone who has done something kind for you.

Today I'm grateful for . . .

MONDAY ___/___/___

TUESDAY ___/___/___

WEDNESDAY ___/___/___

THURSDAY ___/___/___

FRIDAY ___/___/___

SATURDAY ___/___/___

SUNDAY ___/___/___

What was the best part of your week? Describe it below.

"we must find time to stop and thank the people who make a difference in our lives."

—JOHN F. KENNEDY, PRESIDENT

Today I'm grateful for ...

MONDAY ___/___/___

TUESDAY ___/___/___

WEDNESDAY ___/___/___

THURSDAY ___/___/___

FRIDAY ___/___/___

SATURDAY ___/___/___

SUNDAY ___/___/___

What are three nice things that people did for you this week? How did their actions make you feel?

GRATITUDE CHALLENGE!

Pick a spot in your room to hang a photo or drawing of the people you're grateful for.

Today I'm grateful for . . .

MONDAY

____ / ____ / ____

TUESDAY

____ / ____ / ____

WEDNESDAY

____ / ____ / ____

THURSDAY

____ / ____ / ____

FRIDAY

____ / ____ / ____

SATURDAY

____ / ____ / ____

SUNDAY

____ / ____ / ____

Where is your favorite place to go? Draw a picture of it below.

"NO act Of kindness, no matter how small, is ever wasted."

—AESOP, STORYTELLER

Today I'm grateful for ...

MONDAY ____ / ____ / ____

TUESDAY ____ / ____ / ____

WEDNESDAY ____ / ____ / ____

THURSDAY ____ / ____ / ____

FRIDAY ____ / ____ / ____

SATURDAY ____ / ____ / ____

SUNDAY ____ / ____ / ____

Who is your best friend? What do you love about him or her?

_____

_____

_____

_____

_____

_____

_____

GRATITUDE CHALLENGE!

At your next meal, think about all the people who worked to bring you the food you're eating. Discuss it with your family or say a silent thanks to them for their work.

Today I'm grateful for . . .

MONDAY

___ / ___ / ___

TUESDAY

___ / ___ / ___

WEDNESDAY

___ / ___ / ___

THURSDAY

___ / ___ / ___

FRIDAY

___ / ___ / ___

SATURDAY

___ / ___ / ___

SUNDAY

___ / ___ / ___

What did you do to help someone this week? How did you feel afterward?

"If you have good thoughts they will shine out of your face like sunbeams and you will always look lovely."

—ROALD DAHL, AUTHOR

Today I'm grateful for . . .

MONDAY ___/___/___

TUESDAY ___/___/___

WEDNESDAY ___/___/___

THURSDAY ___/___/___

FRIDAY ___/___/___

SATURDAY ___/___/___

SUNDAY ___/___/___

What's your favorite pet? It could be yours or someone else's. Draw a picture of it below.

GRATITUDE CHALLENGE!

Do something nice for someone else, but don't tell them you did it. For example, you could make your brother or sister's bed, or put away the dishes without anyone noticing.

Today I'm grateful for ...

MONDAY ___ / ___ / ___

TUESDAY ___ / ___ / ___

WEDNESDAY ___ / ___ / ___

THURSDAY ___ / ___ / ___

FRIDAY ___ / ___ / ___

SATURDAY ___ / ___ / ___

SUNDAY ___ / ___ / ___

What is your favorite memory? Describe it below.

_____

_____

_____

_____

_____

_____

_____

"If you see someone without a smile, give them one of yours."

—DOLLY PARTON, SINGER

Today I'm grateful for . . .

MONDAY ___ / ___ / ___

TUESDAY ___ / ___ / ___

WEDNESDAY ___ / ___ / ___

THURSDAY ___ / ___ / ___

FRIDAY ___ / ___ / ___

SATURDAY ___ / ___ / ___

SUNDAY ___ / ___ / ___

What is something you are really looking forward to? Why are you so excited about it?

GRATITUDE CHALLENGE!

Hold the door open for someone who has their hands full.

Today I'm grateful for . . .

MONDAY ___ / ___ / ___

TUESDAY ___ / ___ / ___

WEDNESDAY ___ / ___ / ___

THURSDAY ___ / ___ / ___

FRIDAY ___ / ___ / ___

SATURDAY ___ / ___ / ___

SUNDAY ___ / ___ / ___

What do you like best about yourself? Why?

"FOLKS are usually about as happy as
they make their minds up to be."

—ABRAHAM LINCOLN, PRESIDENT

Today I'm grateful for . . .

MONDAY

___ / ___ / ___

TUESDAY

___ / ___ / ___

WEDNESDAY

___ / ___ / ___

THURSDAY

___ / ___ / ___

FRIDAY

___ / ___ / ___

SATURDAY

___ / ___ / ___

SUNDAY

___ / ___ / ___

What is your favorite book? Why do you love it?

_____

_____

_____

_____

_____

_____

_____

_____

23

GRATITUDE CHALLENGE!

Thank someone for something specific. For example, you could thank a friend for helping you with a math problem or a parent for making you lunch.

Today I'm grateful for . . .

MONDAY

___ / ___ / ___

TUESDAY

___ / ___ / ___

WEDNESDAY

___ / ___ / ___

THURSDAY

___ / ___ / ___

FRIDAY

___ / ___ / ___

SATURDAY

___ / ___ / ___

SUNDAY

___ / ___ / ___

What is your favorite spot in your house? What do you like to do there?

"GOOD words are worth much,
and cost little."

—GEORGE HERBERT, POET

Today I'm grateful for ...

MONDAY ___ / ___ / ___

TUESDAY ___ / ___ / ___

WEDNESDAY ___ / ___ / ___

THURSDAY ___ / ___ / ___

FRIDAY ___ / ___ / ___

SATURDAY ___ / ___ / ___

SUNDAY ___ / ___ / ___

Who is the funniest person you know? What do they do that makes you laugh?

_____

_____

_____

_____

_____

_____

_____

GRATITUDE CHALLENGE!

Say hello to someone in your school who you have never talked to before.

Today I'm grateful for . . .

MONDAY ___ / ___ / ___

TUESDAY ___ / ___ / ___

WEDNESDAY ___ / ___ / ___

THURSDAY ___ / ___ / ___

FRIDAY ___ / ___ / ___

SATURDAY ___ / ___ / ___

SUNDAY ___ / ___ / ___

What is one thing in nature that inspires you? Draw it below.

"Learn from yesterday, live for today, hope for tomorrow. The important thing is not to stop questioning."

—ALBERT EINSTEIN, PHYSICIST

Today I'm grateful for . . .

MONDAY ___/___/___

TUESDAY ___/___/___

WEDNESDAY ___/___/___

THURSDAY ___/___/___

FRIDAY ___/___/___

SATURDAY ___/___/___

SUNDAY ___/___/___

What is something new you learned this week? How will it help you?

_____

_____

_____

_____

_____

_____

_____

_____

GRATITUDE CHALLENGE!

Go through toys that you have outgrown and pick five to give to a younger brother, sister, or friend.

Today I'm grateful for . . .

MONDAY

___ / ___ / ___

TUESDAY

___ / ___ / ___

WEDNESDAY

___ / ___ / ___

THURSDAY

___ / ___ / ___

FRIDAY

___ / ___ / ___

SATURDAY

___ / ___ / ___

SUNDAY

___ / ___ / ___

TODAY IS GREAT!

Who are you most grateful for? Who do you think is most grateful for you?

"Life is short, but there is always time for courtesy."

—RALPH WALDO EMERSON, AUTHOR

Today I'm grateful for ...

TODAY IS GREAT!

MONDAY ___ / ___ / ___

TUESDAY ___ / ___ / ___

WEDNESDAY ___ / ___ / ___

THURSDAY ___ / ___ / ___

FRIDAY ___ / ___ / ___

SATURDAY ___ / ___ / ___

SUNDAY ___ / ___ / ___

If you could have your favorite meal for dinner, what would it be? What would you have for dessert?

35

GRATITUDE CHALLENGE!

Write a thank you note to the person who delivers your mail. Leave it in your mailbox for them.

Today I'm grateful for . . .

MONDAY ___ / ___ / ___

TUESDAY ___ / ___ / ___

WEDNESDAY ___ / ___ / ___

THURSDAY ___ / ___ / ___

FRIDAY ___ / ___ / ___

SATURDAY ___ / ___ / ___

SUNDAY ___ / ___ / ___

TODAY IS GREAT!

What is the best vacation you've ever been on? What did you love about it?

"When we give cheerfully and accept gratefully, everyone is blessed."

—MAYA ANGELOU, POET

Today I'm grateful for . . .

MONDAY ___/___/___

TUESDAY ___/___/___

WEDNESDAY ___/___/___

THURSDAY ___/___/___

FRIDAY ___/___/___

SATURDAY ___/___/___

SUNDAY ___/___/___

Draw a self-portrait in the space below. Use a mirror to help you see what you look like.

GRATITUDE CHALLENGE!

Thank the person who does your laundry and offer to help them with it this week.

Today I'm grateful for . . .

TODAY IS GREAT!

MONDAY

___/___/___

TUESDAY

___/___/___

WEDNESDAY

___/___/___

THURSDAY

___/___/___

FRIDAY

___/___/___

SATURDAY

___/___/___

SUNDAY

___/___/___

What is your favorite song? How does it make you feel?

_____

_____

_____

_____

_____

_____

_____

41

"The way to develop the best that is in a person is by appreciation and encouragement."

—CHARLES SCHWAB, INVESTOR

Today I'm grateful for . . .

MONDAY

___/___/___

TUESDAY

___/___/___

WEDNESDAY

___/___/___

THURSDAY

___/___/___

FRIDAY

___/___/___

SATURDAY

___/___/___

SUNDAY

___/___/___

Describe your perfect day. Who would you spend it with? What would you do?

_____

_____

_____

_____

_____

_____

_____

GRATITUDE CHALLENGE!

Write a positive message in sidewalk chalk somewhere a lot of people will see it. For example: "You are special." or "Believe in yourself." or "You are brave."

Today I'm grateful for . . .

MONDAY ___/___/___

TUESDAY ___/___/___

WEDNESDAY ___/___/___

THURSDAY ___/___/___

FRIDAY ___/___/___

SATURDAY ___/___/___

SUNDAY ___/___/___

What do you like best about the way you look? What do you think is the first thing people notice about you?

"Do not let what you cannot do interfere with what you can do."

—JOHN WOODEN, BASKETBALL COACH

Today I'm grateful for ...

MONDAY

___ / ___ / ___

TUESDAY

___ / ___ / ___

WEDNESDAY

___ / ___ / ___

THURSDAY

___ / ___ / ___

FRIDAY

___ / ___ / ___

SATURDAY

___ / ___ / ___

SUNDAY

___ / ___ / ___

Who do you like to talk to when you need help with something? Who is best at cheering you up?

GRATITUDE CHALLENGE!

Count the number of people who smile at you in one day.

Today I'm grateful for . . .

MONDAY   ___ / ___ / ___

TUESDAY   ___ / ___ / ___

WEDNESDAY   ___ / ___ / ___

THURSDAY   ___ / ___ / ___

FRIDAY   ___ / ___ / ___

SATURDAY   ___ / ___ / ___

SUNDAY   ___ / ___ / ___

What is your favorite family tradition? Describe it below.

_____

_____

_____

_____

_____

_____

_____

"Winning doesn't always mean being first. Winning means you're doing better than you've done before."

—BONNIE BLAIR, AMERICAN SPEED SKATER

Today I'm grateful for . . .

MONDAY

___ / ___ / ___

TUESDAY

___ / ___ / ___

WEDNESDAY

___ / ___ / ___

THURSDAY

___ / ___ / ___

FRIDAY

___ / ___ / ___

SATURDAY

___ / ___ / ___

SUNDAY

___ / ___ / ___

Who said something nice to you this week? What did they say? How did it make you feel?

GRATITUDE CHALLENGE!

When you finish reading a book, leave it in a public place, like on a park bench or a bus, for someone else to find. Include a note that says you are passing the book on for someone else to enjoy.

Today I'm grateful for . . .

MONDAY ___ / ___ / ___

TUESDAY ___ / ___ / ___

WEDNESDAY ___ / ___ / ___

THURSDAY ___ / ___ / ___

FRIDAY ___ / ___ / ___

SATURDAY ___ / ___ / ___

SUNDAY ___ / ___ / ___

Describe an act of kindness you witnessed this week.

"In any moment of decision, the best thing you can do is the right thing. The worst thing you can do is nothing."

—THEODORE ROOSEVELT,
PRESIDENT

Today I'm grateful for . . .

MONDAY ___ / ___ / ___

TUESDAY ___ / ___ / ___

WEDNESDAY ___ / ___ / ___

THURSDAY ___ / ___ / ___

FRIDAY ___ / ___ / ___

SATURDAY ___ / ___ / ___

SUNDAY ___ / ___ / ___

What is your favorite thing about each season?

WINTER:

_____

_____

SPRING:

_____

_____

SUMMER:

_____

_____

FALL:

_____

_____

GRATITUDE CHALLENGE!

Offer to clear the table after dinner one night this week.

Today I'm grateful for . . .

MONDAY _____ / _____ / _____

TUESDAY _____ / _____ / _____

WEDNESDAY _____ / _____ / _____

THURSDAY _____ / _____ / _____

FRIDAY _____ / _____ / _____

SATURDAY _____ / _____ / _____

SUNDAY _____ / _____ / _____

What is your favorite thing to do outside? Describe it below.

_____

_____

_____

_____

_____

_____

_____

57

"Yesterday is history. Tomorrow is a mystery. Today is a gift. That's why we call it 'The Present.'"

—ELEANOR ROOSEVELT, FIRST LADY

Today I'm grateful for . . .

TODAY IS GREAT!

MONDAY

___ / ___ / ___

TUESDAY

___ / ___ / ___

WEDNESDAY

___ / ___ / ___

THURSDAY

___ / ___ / ___

FRIDAY

___ / ___ / ___

SATURDAY

___ / ___ / ___

SUNDAY

___ / ___ / ___

Describe your family. What makes it special?

_____

_____

_____

_____

_____

_____

_____

GRATITUDE CHALLENGE!

Do something nice for a teacher, like drawing them a picture, bringing in a treat, or offering to help with something in their classroom.

Today I'm grateful for . . .

MONDAY ___ / ___ / ___

TUESDAY ___ / ___ / ___

WEDNESDAY ___ / ___ / ___

THURSDAY ___ / ___ / ___

FRIDAY ___ / ___ / ___

SATURDAY ___ / ___ / ___

SUNDAY ___ / ___ / ___

TODAY IS GREAT!

What are five words your friends would use to describe you?

_____

_____

_____

_____

_____

"Be silly. Be honest. Be kind."

—RALPH WALDO EMERSON, AUTHOR

Today I'm grateful for . . .

MONDAY ___/___/___

TUESDAY ___/___/___

WEDNESDAY ___/___/___

THURSDAY ___/___/___

FRIDAY ___/___/___

SATURDAY ___/___/___

SUNDAY ___/___/___

What is your favorite sport to play? What is your favorite sport to watch? Why do you like them?

GRATITUDE CHALLENGE!

Look for a classmate who is eating lunch alone, and invite them to join you.

Today I'm grateful for ...

MONDAY

___ / ___ / ___

TUESDAY

___ / ___ / ___

WEDNESDAY

___ / ___ / ___

THURSDAY

___ / ___ / ___

FRIDAY

___ / ___ / ___

SATURDAY

___ / ___ / ___

SUNDAY

___ / ___ / ___

What three things that you own do you value the most?

_____

_____

_____

_____

_____

_____

_____

"Without the rain, there would be no rainbow."

—G.K. CHESTERTON, AUTHOR

Today I'm grateful for . . .

MONDAY

____ / ____ / ____

TUESDAY

____ / ____ / ____

WEDNESDAY

____ / ____ / ____

THURSDAY

____ / ____ / ____

FRIDAY

____ / ____ / ____

SATURDAY

____ / ____ / ____

SUNDAY

____ / ____ / ____

What is your favorite smell? When and where do you usually smell it?

GRATITUDE CHALLENGE!

Write some positive messages on sticky notes and stick them up around the house where your family will see them. You can write things like "You're the best!" and "I love you!"

Today I'm grateful for . . .

MONDAY _____ / _____ / _____

TUESDAY _____ / _____ / _____

WEDNESDAY _____ / _____ / _____

THURSDAY _____ / _____ / _____

FRIDAY _____ / _____ / _____

SATURDAY _____ / _____ / _____

SUNDAY _____ / _____ / _____

Describe a time when someone helped you solve a problem. Who was it? How did they help you?

"Be thankful for what you have; you'll end up having more. If you concentrate on what you don't have, you will never, ever have enough."

—OPRAH WINFREY, MEDIA EXECUTIVE

Today I'm grateful for ...

MONDAY
___ / ___ / ___

TUESDAY
___ / ___ / ___

WEDNESDAY
___ / ___ / ___

THURSDAY
___ / ___ / ___

FRIDAY
___ / ___ / ___

SATURDAY
___ / ___ / ___

SUNDAY
___ / ___ / ___

TODAY IS GREAT!

Describe a time when someone surprised you with kindness. What did they do, and how did it make you feel?

_____

_____

_____

_____

_____

_____

_____

GRATITUDE CHALLENGE!

Tell a family member or friend what you like about them.

Today I'm grateful for . . .

MONDAY ___/___/___

TUESDAY ___/___/___

WEDNESDAY ___/___/___

THURSDAY ___/___/___

FRIDAY ___/___/___

SATURDAY ___/___/___

SUNDAY ___/___/___

Which of your five senses (sight, hearing, touch, taste, smell) are you the most grateful for? Why?

_____

_____

_____

_____

_____

_____

_____

"Carry out a random act of kindness,
with no expectation of reward,
safe in the knowledge that one day
someone might do the same for you."

—DIANA, PRINCESS OF WALES

Today I'm grateful for ...

MONDAY   ___/___/___

TUESDAY   ___/___/___

WEDNESDAY   ___/___/___

THURSDAY   ___/___/___

FRIDAY   ___/___/___

SATURDAY   ___/___/___

SUNDAY   ___/___/___

What was the best birthday you've ever had? Why was it so great?

_____

_____

_____

_____

_____

_____

_____

_____

GRATITUDE CHALLENGE!

Ask an adult to take you to a local park. Bring a garbage bag and gloves, and pick up any trash you find there.

Today I'm grateful for . . .

MONDAY ___ / ___ / ___

TUESDAY ___ / ___ / ___

WEDNESDAY ___ / ___ / ___

THURSDAY ___ / ___ / ___

FRIDAY ___ / ___ / ___

SATURDAY ___ / ___ / ___

SUNDAY ___ / ___ / ___

Pick one family member. It could be a parent, sibling, grandparent, or other relative. How does he or she make your life better?

"The time is always right to do what is right."

—MARTIN LUTHER KING JR.,
MINISTER AND ACTIVIST

Today I'm grateful for . . .

MONDAY ___/___/___

TUESDAY ___/___/___

WEDNESDAY ___/___/___

THURSDAY ___/___/___

FRIDAY ___/___/___

SATURDAY ___/___/___

SUNDAY ___/___/___

What is your favorite holiday? What do you do to celebrate it?

GRATITUDE CHALLENGE!

With an adult's help, bake brownies and hand them out to your neighbors.

Today I'm grateful for . . .

MONDAY

_____ / _____ / _____

TUESDAY

_____ / _____ / _____

WEDNESDAY

_____ / _____ / _____

THURSDAY

_____ / _____ / _____

FRIDAY

_____ / _____ / _____

SATURDAY

_____ / _____ / _____

SUNDAY

_____ / _____ / _____

TODAY IS GREAT!

What teacher has made the biggest difference in your life? What did they do that was so special?

_____

_____

_____

_____

_____

_____

_____

"Friendship is born at that moment when one person says to another, 'What! You too? I thought I was the only one.'"

—C. S. LEWIS, WRITER

Today I'm grateful for . . .

MONDAY

_____ / _____ / _____

TUESDAY

_____ / _____ / _____

WEDNESDAY

_____ / _____ / _____

THURSDAY

_____ / _____ / _____

FRIDAY

_____ / _____ / _____

SATURDAY

_____ / _____ / _____

SUNDAY

_____ / _____ / _____

What was the most delicious thing you ate this week? Who made it for you? What made it so good?

_____

_____

_____

_____

_____

_____

_____

GRATITUDE CHALLENGE!

Compliment three people on something they have done well.

Today I'm grateful for . . .

MONDAY ___/___/___

TUESDAY ___/___/___

WEDNESDAY ___/___/___

THURSDAY ___/___/___

FRIDAY ___/___/___

SATURDAY ___/___/___

SUNDAY ___/___/___

What subject in school do you enjoy most? What do you like about it?

"The only way to have a friend is to be one."

—RALPH WALDO EMERSON, AUTHOR

Today I'm grateful for . . .

MONDAY ___ / ___ / ___

TUESDAY ___ / ___ / ___

WEDNESDAY ___ / ___ / ___

THURSDAY ___ / ___ / ___

FRIDAY ___ / ___ / ___

SATURDAY ___ / ___ / ___

SUNDAY ___ / ___ / ___

When was the last time you said "I love you"? Who did you say it to?

GRATITUDE CHALLENGE!

Offer to help someone in class who is struggling with a subject you're good at.

Today I'm grateful for . . .

MONDAY ___ / ___ / ___

TUESDAY ___ / ___ / ___

WEDNESDAY ___ / ___ / ___

THURSDAY ___ / ___ / ___

FRIDAY ___ / ___ / ___

SATURDAY ___ / ___ / ___

SUNDAY ___ / ___ / ___

TODAY IS GREAT!

What was the best gift you have ever received?
Was it something you had wanted for a long
time or a surprise that you ended up loving?

"The more you like yourself,
the less you are like anyone else,
which makes you unique."

—WALT DISNEY, ANIMATOR

Today I'm grateful for . . .

TODAY IS GREAT!

MONDAY

___ / ___ / ___

TUESDAY

___ / ___ / ___

WEDNESDAY

___ / ___ / ___

THURSDAY

___ / ___ / ___

FRIDAY

___ / ___ / ___

SATURDAY

___ / ___ / ___

SUNDAY

___ / ___ / ___

What can you do to brighten someone's day tomorrow?

_____

_____

_____

_____

_____

_____

_____

GRATITUDE CHALLENGE!

Invite a new friend to hang out with you. This could be someone in your class that you don't know very well or someone who just moved to your neighborhood.

Today I'm grateful for . . .

MONDAY ___ / ___ / ___

TUESDAY ___ / ___ / ___

WEDNESDAY ___ / ___ / ___

THURSDAY ___ / ___ / ___

FRIDAY ___ / ___ / ___

SATURDAY ___ / ___ / ___

SUNDAY ___ / ___ / ___

Describe a time when you were brave.
What did you do? Was it easy or hard?

_____

_____

_____

_____

_____

_____

_____

"We do not need magic to transform the world. We carry all the power we need inside ourselves already. We have the power to imagine better."

—J. K. ROWLING, WRITER

Today I'm grateful for . . .

TODAY IS GREAT!

MONDAY

___ / ___ / ___

TUESDAY

___ / ___ / ___

WEDNESDAY

___ / ___ / ___

THURSDAY

___ / ___ / ___

FRIDAY

___ / ___ / ___

SATURDAY

___ / ___ / ___

SUNDAY

___ / ___ / ___

What time of day do you like best: mornings, afternoons, or evenings? What do you like to do during that time?

_____

_____

_____

_____

_____

_____

_____

_____

GRATITUDE CHALLENGE!

Ask a grandparent or older relative what they liked to do for fun when they were your age.

Today I'm grateful for . . .

MONDAY

___ / ___ / ___

TUESDAY

___ / ___ / ___

WEDNESDAY

___ / ___ / ___

THURSDAY

___ / ___ / ___

FRIDAY

___ / ___ / ___

SATURDAY

___ / ___ / ___

SUNDAY

___ / ___ / ___

What is your favorite way to exercise?
For example, it could be running, dancing,
or playing soccer.

"Kind words can be short
and easy to speak, but their
echoes are truly endless."

—MOTHER TERESA, HUMANITARIAN

Today I'm grateful for . . .

MONDAY ___/___/___

TUESDAY ___/___/___

WEDNESDAY ___/___/___

THURSDAY ___/___/___

FRIDAY ___/___/___

SATURDAY ___/___/___

SUNDAY ___/___/___

What made you laugh this week? Why was it so funny?

GRATITUDE CHALLENGE!

Tell three people your favorite joke.

Today I'm grateful for . . .

MONDAY

___/___/___

TUESDAY

___/___/___

WEDNESDAY

___/___/___

THURSDAY

___/___/___

FRIDAY

___/___/___

SATURDAY

___/___/___

SUNDAY

___/___/___

What is your favorite hobby? What do you like about it?

"When I started counting my blessings, my whole life turned around."

—WILLIE NELSON, MUSICIAN

Today I'm grateful for . . .

MONDAY ___ / ___ / ___

TUESDAY ___ / ___ / ___

WEDNESDAY ___ / ___ / ___

THURSDAY ___ / ___ / ___

FRIDAY ___ / ___ / ___

SATURDAY ___ / ___ / ___

SUNDAY ___ / ___ / ___

TODAY IS GREAT!

What do you love the most about your life?

_____

_____

_____

_____

_____

_____

_____

GRATITUDE CHALLENGE!

With an adult's help, collect food to donate to a local soup kitchen or shelter.

Today I'm grateful for . . .

TODAY IS GREAT!

MONDAY

___ / ___ / ___

TUESDAY

___ / ___ / ___

WEDNESDAY

___ / ___ / ___

THURSDAY

___ / ___ / ___

FRIDAY

___ / ___ / ___

SATURDAY

___ / ___ / ___

SUNDAY

___ / ___ / ___

What do you like most about keeping a gratitude journal? How has it helped you?

"It always seems impossible until it is done."

—NELSON MANDELA, POLITICAL LEADER

ABOUT THE AUTHOR

Vicky Perreault is the founder of *Mess for Less* (www.messforless.net) where she shares kids' activities, parenting tips, and family-friendly recipes. She is a former teacher who holds a master's degree in early childhood and elementary education. She uses that experience to create fun learning opportunities for her children and her blog readers. Vicky is the mom of three amazing girls and the wife of the best husband anyone could ask for. She is grateful for them all.

Thank You!

CPSIA information can be obtained
at www.ICGtesting.com
Printed in the USA
BVHW020418281219
567609BV00002BB/3/P

9 781641 528825